Daily Journal

Who I am in Christ

property of:

_____

Ways to use this Journal

Write out prayers

Meditation & insights

Gratitude & blessings

Connecting with your

emotions

Reflect on identity words and

scriptures provided

For help discovering your identity in Christ, access this free tool: Identity Compass
https://www.katherinemaclaren.com/identity-compass/

I Am Chosen

"You did not choose me, but I chose you and appointed you that you should go and bear fruit and that your fruit should abide, so that whatever you ask the Father in my name, he may give it to you."
John 15:16

I Am Blessed

"Praise be to the God and Father of our Lord Jesus Christ, who has blessed us in the heavenly realms with every spiritual blessing in Christ." Ephesians 1:3

I Am a Child of God

"See what great love the Father has lavished on us, that we should be called children of God! And that is what we are!" 1John 3:1

I Am Fully Known

"Lord, you have searched me and you know me. You know when I sit and when I rise; you perceive my thoughts from afar. You discern my going out and my lying down; you are familiar with all my ways. Before a word is on my tongue you know it completely." Psalm 139:1-4

I Am a Light

"Then Jesus said, "I am the light of the world, and those who embrace me will experience life-giving light, and they will never walk in darkness." John 8:12

I Am a New Creation

"Therefore, if anyone is in Christ, he is a new creation. The old has passed away; behold, the new has come." 2 Corinthians 5:17

I Am Redeemed

"Fear not, for I have redeemed you; I have called you by name, you are mine." Isaiah 43:1

I Am Accepted

"To the praise of his glorious grace, by which he made us accepted in the Beloved." Ephesians 1:6

I Am God's Masterpiece

"For we are God's masterpiece. He has created us anew in Christ Jesus, so we can do the good things he planned for us long ago." Ephesians 2:10

I Am Saved by Grace

"For by grace you have been saved through faith. And this is not your own doing; it is the gift of God..." Ephesians 2:8

I Am Strong

"Therefore I will boast all the more gladly about my weaknesses, so that Christ's power may rest on me. That is why for Christ's sake, I delight in weaknesses...for when I am weak, then I am strong." 2 Corinthians 12:10

I Am Alive in Christ

"But because of his great love for us, God, who is rich in mercy, made us alive with Christ even when we were dead in our transgressions - it is by grace you have been saved." Ephesians 2:4-5

I Am Raised With Christ

"And God raised us up with Christ and seated us with him in the heavenly realms in Christ Jesus."
Ephesians 2:6

I Am a Citizen of Heaven

"But our citizenship is in heaven..." Philippians 3:20

I Am Forgiven

"In him we have redemption through his blood, the forgiveness of sins, in accordance with the riches of God's grace." Ephesians 1:7

I Am Predestined

"In love he predestined us for adoption to sonship through Jesus Christ, in accordance with his pleasure and will..." Ephesians 1:5

I Am an Ambassador

"Therefore, we are ambassadors for Christ, God making his appeal through us. We implore you on behalf of Christ, be reconciled to God."
2 Corinthians 5:20

I Am Bold

"For the Spirit God gave us does not make us timid, but gives us power, love and self-discipline."
2Timothy 1:7

I Am a Disciple

"By this all people will know that you are my disciples, if you have love for one another."
John 13:35

I Am Sustained

"And my God will meet all your needs according to the riches of his glory in Christ Jesus."
Philippians 4:19

I Am Free

"Then you will know the truth, and the truth will set you free." John 8:32

I Am Secure

"I give them eternal life, and they shall never perish; no one will snatch them out of my hand."
John 10:28

I Am Unique

"You made all of the delicate, inner parts of my body and knit me together in my mother's womb."
Psalms 139:13

I Am Loved

"And I am convinced that nothing can ever separate us from God's love..." Romans 8:38-39

I Am Confident

"But blessed is the one who trusts in the Lord, whose confidence is in him." Jeremiah 17:7

I Am an Heir

"And since we are his children, we are his heirs. In fact, together with Christ we are heirs of God's glory." Romans 8:17

I Am Justified

"Therefore, since we have been justified by faith, we have peace with God through our Lord Jesus Christ..."
Romans 5:1

I Am Precious

"Since you are precious and honored in my sight, and because I love you, I will give people in exchange for you, nations in exchange for your life." Isaiah 43:4

I Am Valuable

"Why, even the hairs of your head are all numbered. Fear not; you are of more value than many sparrows." Luke 12:7

I Am Significant

"So God created man in his own image, in the image of God he created him; male and female he created them." Genesis 1:27

I Am Victorious

"But thanks be to God, who gives us the victory through our Lord Jesus Christ." 1 Corinthians 15:57

I Am Never Alone

"It is the Lord who goes before you. He will be with you: he will not leave you or forsake you. Do not fear or be dismayed." Deuteronomy 31:8

I Am a Saint

"So then you are no longer strangers and aliens, but you are fellow citizens with the saints and members of the household of God." Ephesians 2:19

I Am Safe

"In peace I will lie down and sleep, for you alone, Lord, make me dwell in safety." Psalm 4:8

I Am a Conqueror

"No, in all these things we are more than conquerors through him who loved us." Romans 8:37

I Am His Beloved

"To the praise of his glorious grace, with which he has blessed us in the Beloved." Ephesians 1:6

I Am a Delight

"He will take great delight in you. He will rejoice
over you with singing." Zephaniah 3:17

I Am Sanctified

"Sanctify them by the truth; your word is truth."
John 17:17

I Am Protected

"My prayer is not that you take them out of the world but that you protect them from the evil one."
John 17:15

I Am Anointed

"But the anointing that you received from him abides in you, and you have no need that anyone should teach you..." 1 John 2:27

I Am Wonderful

"I praise you, for I am fearfully and wonderfully made. Wonderful are your works; my soul knows it very well." Psalm 139:14

I Am Seen

"For the eyes of the Lord are on the righteous and his ears are attentive to their prayer..." 1 Peter 3:12

I Am Heard

"When the righteous cry for help, the Lord hears and delivers them out of all their troubles."
Psalm 34:17

I Am Complete

"For in Christ all the fullness of the Deity lives in bodily form, and in Christ you have been brought to fullness. He is the head over every power and authority." Colossians 2:10

I Am His Friend

"I no longer call you servants, because a servant does not know his master's business. Instead, I have called you friends, for everything that I learned from my Father I have made known to you." John 15:15

I Am Sealed by God

"And it is God who establishes us with you in Christ, and has anointed us, and who has also put his seal on us and given us his Spirit in our hearts as a guarantee." 2 Corinthians 1:21-22

I Am Righteous

"For our sake he made him to be sin who knew no sin, so that in him we might become the righteousness of God." 2 Corinthians 5:21

I Am Empowered

"But you will receive power when my Holy Spirit has come upon you..." Acts 1:8

I Am Able

"Now to him who is able to do immeasurably more than all we ask or imagine, according to his power that is at work within us." Ephesians 3:20

I Am Hidden with Christ

"For you have died, and your life is now hidden with Christ in God." Colossians 3:3

I Am Born of God

"Everyone who believes that Jesus is the Christ is born of God..." 1 John 5:1

I Am God's Co-Worker

"As God's co-workers we urge you not to receive
God's grace in vain."
2 Corinthians 6:1

I Am Fruitful

"But the fruit of the Spirit is love, joy, peace, patience, kindness, goodness, faithfulness, gentleness, self-control; against such things there is no law." Galatians 5:22-23

I Am Gifted

"Each of you should use whatever gift you have received to serve others, as faithful stewards of God's grace in its various forms." 1 Peter 4:10

I Am Above

"The Lord will make you the head, not the tail. If you pay attention to the commands of the Lord your God that I give you this day and carefully follow them, you will always be at the top, never at the bottom." Deuteronomy 28:13

I Am Treasured

"Out of all the peoples on the face of the earth, the Lord has chosen you to be his treasured possession." Deuteronomy 14:2

I Am Set Apart

"But you are a chosen race, a royal priesthood, a holy nation, God's special possession, that you may declare the praises of him who called you out of darkness into his wonderful light." 1 Peter 2:9

I Am Triumphant

"But thanks be to God, who in Christ always leads us in triumphal procession, and through us spreads the fragrance of the knowledge of him everywhere." 2 Corinthians 2:14

I Am God's Temple

"Do you not know that you are God's temple and that God's Spirit dwells in you?" 1 Corinthians 3:16